CAREER IN MARKETING

BRAND MANAGER

SOME OF THE MOST REWARDING AND challenging careers today are available in the marketing specialty of brand management. Brand managers are primarily responsible for the marketing activities for a certain brand to increase its market share, boost profitability, and ensure consumers in its target markets view it favorably. The brand manager is the executive who monitors market trends to ensure products and services align with the brand's image. Brand managers take responsibility for the success or failure of one or more brands (such as Coca-Cola or Toyota), weighing such factors as consumer perception, financial performance, and the brand's image around the world. Brands are not always products and services. They can also be organizations, nonprofit causes, or even individuals (such as celebrities and professional athletes).

Brand managers typically work for large corporations and marketing firms in major metropolitan areas, although they are also found in cities of all sizes across the country. The career of brand management is commonly found in consumer goods manufacturers, software companies, airlines, financial services companies, universities, and professional sports. Brand marketing professionals also work for advertising agencies, media firms, nonprofit organizations, and government agencies.

Some brand managers are self-employed and operate their own consultancy firms.

A four-year degree from an accredited college or university is typically the minimum requirement to begin a career in the brand management field. A graduate degree is usually required to obtain a position as an assistant brand manager, and is mandatory for a marketing brand manager. Many brand managers enter the profession at such entry-level positions as marketing analyst or brand ambassador, and can rise as high as marketing director in a company.

The number of marketing management jobs is expected to grow by about 15 percent within the coming decade, roughly the average employment growth among most professions. The need for marketing brand managers will continue to climb as new products and services are introduced, and as companies take steps to strengthen existing brands.

Marketing managers (which includes brand managers) earn on average about $130,000 annually.

Would you be successful as a marketing brand manager? Some technical training is required to learn the strategies and techniques of brand management, but personal traits are equally important for success. Do you communicate well speaking and in writing? Are you creative? Do you like working in a collaborative environment with different types of people to achieve a common goal? Would you be comfortable in a leadership role?

If you have good analytical, interpersonal, and technical skills, you can enjoy a financially rewarding career as a marketing brand manager. The hours can be long and stressful. Brand managers are responsible for all facets of a brand — from advertising and promotion through packaging and design – so managers need to be adept at dealing with all aspects of business administration. Through proper training, hard work, and solid personal traits, you can achieve the personal and professional satisfaction that many marketing brand managers enjoy.

WHAT YOU CAN DO NOW

EVEN WHILE YOU ARE STILL IN HIGH school, you can take steps to prepare for a career as a marketing brand manager. Start with English and speech courses to enhance your communications skills. If your school has classes in marketing, advertising, graphic design, communications, or media, sign up!

Promotions are part of brand marketing, so volunteer to handle publicity for your clubs and other organizations. Serve on your high school newspaper or yearbook staff. Submit school news stories to local publications, TV and radio stations, and community bulletin boards online. Look for leadership opportunities when you volunteer, as these will help you prepare for a management role. Getting some experience in sales – at school or in a part-time job – will also be valuable.

Using new technologies is another critical component to the marketing career path. Classes on word processing software, computer graphics, web design, videography, and desktop publishing tools can be useful. If you are unable to find the right classes at your school, look at local colleges and universities. Online courses can also provide great learning opportunities at little or no cost. Social media is increasingly important for brand managers, so experiment with Facebook, Twitter, Pinterest, LinkedIn, YouTube, and similar platforms.

Begin learning about marketing and brand management by reading industry periodicals, visiting professional association websites, and checking the business section of your newspaper to stay up-to-date with industry trends. Attend local chapter meetings of professional marketing associations and find out what student memberships they offer. Many groups offer scholarships or help match interns with employers, so getting involved in a professional association early can help you improve your chances to land those vital opportunities later on.

HISTORY OF THE CAREER

THE PRACTICE OF BRANDING HAS ITS origins in ancient times. Early craftsmen would put a distinctive, individual mark on handmade goods that identified the person who had created a certain piece of pottery or jewelry. As early as 2700 BC, Egyptians marked their farm animals with a distinctive mark that identified ownership. Japanese businesses used a seal known as a *mon* to distinguish their products from competitors.

In Western Europe, branding began in Sweden during the Middle Ages as a way to identify farm commodities. Vikings burned symbols of Norse gods into their animals to show ownership. The Vikings brought their *brandr* to England, where it was shortened to *brand* and was known in trade law as *trademark*. In 1474, Venetian patent law recognized trademarks, setting legal precedence for their legal protection.

By the 19th century, brands were common to distinguish products made by different manufacturers. The earliest brands were used in the 18th century to identify beverages under such trade names as Twinings (tea), Schweppes (carbonated waters and ginger ales), and Ballantine's (Scotch whiskey), that remain in use more than 200 years later. The Industrial Revolution of the mid-1800s saw brands spreading to consumer goods, such as Levi's and Heinz. Improved transportation later in that century spread brands to new domestic and international markets, promoting such brand names as Ivory soap and Coca-Cola. Consumer goods companies soon began building their advertising around brand names, further distinguishing their products.

The practice we know today as brand management began at Procter & Gamble (P&G) in 1931 with Neil McElroy, who was in charge of advertising for Camay soap. He realized he was competing not only with other soap companies like Lever and Palmolive, but also against other P&G products like Ivory. McElroy wrote a memo to his bosses arguing that the company should form brand management teams who would be responsible for a single brand, not just its advertising, but for its marketing, sales, public relations, promotions, research and development, and even manufacturing and logistics. He advocated an approach in which each brand would be run like its own separate division, allowing the brand to develop its own consumer base. McElroy's idea was embraced first by P&G. After early success, brand management spread to other consumer goods companies, and eventually to all types of products. The growth of the service economy after World War II soon brought brand management to services as well.

During the 1970s, the concepts of brand management evolved further as more companies favored marketing over advertising. Advertising refers to paid non-personal announcements, while marketing is a broader mix of business tools that includes public relations, corporate sponsorships, and other activities that raise awareness of a company's products and services. Branding is marketing for a specific brand, establishing a relationship with customers, and communicating the values associated with a brand (such as "Coke adds life" and "The pause that refreshes").

For centuries, sales of a product had been driven solely by the quality of that product. However, even high quality products could no longer compete successfully unless they could project a brand image that connected with the consumers who were targeted as potential customers. Marketing communications would help position a particular brand in the minds of consumers. For example, they would think of General Motors' Lincoln Town Car as a high-quality luxury automobile, and the Chevy Chevette as a low-cost, dependable, no-frills car.

By the 1980s, the value of successful brand management became quantified in the concept of brand equity. How much is a brand worth? Different methods arose to determine the value of a brand. For example, when Phillip Morris paid $12.6 billion for Kraft Foods in 1988, a significant portion of that purchase price was attributed to the value of the Kraft brand in the marketplace. Experts soon developed models for building and valuing brand equity for products and services of all types, and brands came to be considered a corporate asset.

In 2000, Interbrand, a global corporate identity and branding consultant, released its first ranking of the most valuable brands in the world. Coca-Cola topped the "Best Global Brands" in 2000 and held the leading spot for more than a decade. However, technology companies began to outpace consumer goods in brand equity. In 2013, Apple and Google surpassed Coca-Cola as the top global brand. Interbrand estimated the Apple brand's value at $98.3 billion, a 28 percent increase in just one year over 2012. The brand value at Coca-Cola had risen only two percent to $79.2 billion. The top 10 brands for 2013 also included IBM, Microsoft, Samsung and Intel.

The Internet revolution of the early 21st century not only established new brand value leaders, it also created new challenges and opportunities for brand management. Earlier brand campaigns had focused on print and TV advertising, publicity, celebrity tie-ins and sponsorships. New technology created new platforms that affected brand values. Print and traditional media advertising collapsed during the global recession that began in 2008, pushing more marketing dollars to website advertising. Social media such as Facebook and Twitter presented new avenues for brand managers to promote their products – and new challenges when consumers posted their own opinions about goods and services. Smartphone and tablet applications (apps) provided new ways to get a brand's name in front of tech-savvy consumers.

Brand managers going forward face a variety of interconnected platforms that continue to expand the ways a brand interacts with consumers.

WHERE YOU WILL WORK

WHILE THE DISCIPLINE OF BRAND management originated in consumer goods companies, marketing brand managers are now found in all types of industries, as well as at government agencies and nonprofit institutions. Software companies, airlines, mobile phone carriers, hardware manufacturers, and many other businesses employ professionals to maintain the brand equity of their products and services. Many brand managers work for large corporations, with others found at marketing companies, advertising agencies, public relations firms and similar media-oriented businesses. Some are self-employed and work with a variety of clients on branding projects.

Marketing brand managers typically work in modern, clean, and environmentally friendly offices, either at corporate headquarters or at branch offices around the country. The states with the highest level of employment for marketing managers are California, New York, Texas, Illinois and New Jersey. Top metropolitan areas with the most marketing managers include cities located in those states, as well as Boston, Seattle, Atlanta, San Francisco, Minneapolis and Washington, DC. Some managers also work at least part of the time from their homes as telecommuters.

While brand managers work long hours at their offices, they may also travel for business. Managers may have to visit other divisions of the company, such as the plant where products are manufactured. They may make presentations at industry conferences or call on clients in the US or overseas. Brand managers who are self-employed or work for marketing consulting firms travel frequently between the offices of their clients for meetings and presentations.

Brand managers work in almost every industry. All companies need marketing assistance, especially those that have one or more brands in the marketplace. A recent survey found that marketing brand managers earn the highest salaries in the consumer goods sector. Brand managers also typically work more than 40 hours per week, including nights, weekends and holidays.

THE WORK YOU WILL DO

A MARKETING BRAND MANAGER IS A corporate executive responsible for building the profitability of a company's brand. Brands are used to identify products or services, such as Starbucks Coffee and AT&T Wireless. The brand manager is charged with cultivating the brand's identity, making sure it reflects the image and values that are desirable to the consumers being targeted for the brand. The ultimate goal of brand management is to enhance the brand's position in the marketplace, differentiating it from competing products and services in order to increase sales and profit.

While brand management is primarily a marketing communications function, brand managers must also work with all parts of the company. Brand managers typically function like small business owners within a larger organization, taking responsibility for one or more brands within the enterprise. Managing a brand requires collaboration and cooperation across different departments within an organization. Branding is more than a memorable logo or a catchy slogan. Marketing brand managers must ensure that packaging, product quality, pricing, customer service, distribution and shipping, advertising, and all other activities that affect the customer's experience accurately reflect the image associated with that brand.

Brand managers typically enter the profession with a four-year degree in marketing, business administration, or a similar degree. They often begin their careers as marketing researchers or assistants, moving up to assistant brand manager, and eventually brand manager within a company. A graduate MBA degree (Master of Business Administration) is often required for a brand manager position.

The daily duties of a marketing brand manager vary among industries and among individual companies. In general, brand managers plan, develop and direct marketing campaigns for a particular product or service. They may work to introduce a new brand, or to enhance an existing brand.

Brand managers begin by doing research on existing brands and on what competitors are doing in the marketplace. They use the results to begin developing strategic campaigns that support the brand's image with targeted consumer groups. Market research is conducted and analyzed to test possible approaches to brand image enhancement. Brand managers also review the results of previous campaigns to help determine what changes in approach could be helpful in the current marketplace. Statistical analysis and test markets are used to further develop the strategy and gauge the potential effectiveness of the campaign. Beyond numerical research, brand managers must also be creative to devise original approaches to help build their brands.

The resulting brand strategy is then transformed into tactics for a marketing campaign to promote the brand. The brand manager may work with advertising agencies, production companies, graphic designers, photographers and videographers, copywriters, packaging specialists, digital marketers, public relations firms, social media experts, mobile marketing consultants, and similar creative professionals to bring the campaign to life.

Once the campaign begins, the brand manager must follow up constantly to make sure the desired results are being obtained. Increased sales provide an obvious indicator that a branding campaign is succeeding. Managers also conduct extensive marketing research to determine how consumers perceive the brand, and whether that image is being enhanced and strengthened by the marketing campaign. The management team may modify their approach or change their marketing mix (such as favoring social media over print ads), depending on the results.

Brand Ambassadors

Some future marketing brand managers start their careers as brand ambassadors. The role of brand ambassadors is strictly tactical. They promote and demonstrate existing products at public events, and through such platforms as email marketing and social media. They help implement strategies that are already in place. Working as a brand ambassador (or on sales teams) gives marketing professionals valuable personal experience in what it takes to bring a brand's promise to life in the real world.

Marketing Analyst

While working as a salesperson or brand ambassador does not require any special education, gaining employment as an analyst or researcher does require at least a four-year college degree. Marketing analysts and marketing researchers are typically recent graduates who support the efforts of one or more brand managers. The analyst may work exclusively on one brand, or may be part of a team that works on several brands.

Marketing analysts are more focused on the execution of brand strategy than in developing that strategy. They spend most of their time looking at market research data and summarizing information to let others know whether the brand strategy is successful. They may put together spreadsheets, track budgeted expenses against actual costs, break down sales results by consumer traits, proofread advertising copy, or create PowerPoint slides summarizing their analysis of the competition.

Assistant Brand Manager

After a few years as a marketing analyst, the next step on the career ladder is assistant brand manager (ABM). The ABM position usually requires an MBA, preferably in branding, marketing or another business function.

An ABM may have responsibility for one individual brand within a larger group of brands that are overseen by a brand manager. However, the ABM will often work on several brands and coordinate teams that bring together different corporate departments (such as finance, manufacturing, advertising, and research and development). The brand manager has ultimate responsibility for setting brand strategy, but the ABM frequently has considerable input into those decisions. The ABM also functions as the advocate who makes sure the branding message is followed throughout the entire company or organization.

Typical ABMs manage analysts and administrative staff members, oversee research projects, and track marketing plans against brand performance results (such as sales volume and profitability). Much of their day is spent answering emails and voice mails, participating in cross-company meetings, reviewing the work of other team members, and continually learning more about the business and their industry. The role of an ABM provides an opportunity for someone to demonstrate management, technical and leadership skills, while preparing for promotion to a position of higher responsibility.

Brand Manager

About half of ABMs move up to brand manager. The BM is responsible for a major brand (such as Diet Coke), or sometimes a portfolio of several smaller brands (such as Sprite and Sprite Zero). The brand manager directly supervises a team of ABMs, and is responsible for all the marketing analysts, researchers, and similar direct marketing staff who work on that brand. At many companies, supervising and mentoring those subordinates is a major duty of the brand manager, as corporations prefer to develop their own talent internally and promote from their current staff. A large portion of the brand manager's compensation is typically tied to the performance of the brand they manage, as well as to the company's overall financial results.

Another major difference between ABMs and brand managers is that the ABMs are still largely working on tactics, even as they learn the details of developing a brand strategy. In contrast, the brand manager is in a mostly strategic role.

Devising or modifying brand strategy calls for sound analytical skills plus creative imagination. The brand manager may have developed the initial brand strategy, or may be charged with upgrading the strategy introduced by someone else. In either case, the methodology for developing a brand strategy is basically the same.

Marketing brand managers begin by identifying the brand's target customers, the ones that are most important to the success of the service or product. They must understand those customers' motivations in choosing their brand over a competitor's offerings in the marketplace. Successful brand managers need to not only understand the demographics of their most important customers, but also be able to "get inside their heads," to understand their thought process in choosing one brand over another.

The brand manager next identifies how the brand is positioned in the market (or for a new product, where it should be positioned). Is it a high-price luxury item that appeals to wealthy consumers, for example, or an inexpensive product whose main selling point is a lower retail price? Branding focuses on a customer's emotional connection to the product or service, so brand positioning also calls for building a brand image that reinforces the reasons a consumer identifies with that brand. Overall, the manager wants to position the brand to give the company the greatest advantages in the marketplace and build up brand equity – the economic value of that brand.

Brand positioning drives the more tactical approaches of marketing. The goal is building an identity that reflects the values consumers seek and the promises the company wants that brand to make to customers who buy the product or service. This "brand promise" needs to be reflected and reinforced through brand messaging, the product's appearance, consumer experiences using the product, advertising, customer service — any other point where consumers interact with the brand.

After the brand manager devises a strategy built around brand identity and brand promise, that strategy must be sold to upper management. Once the marketing director and other executives approve that strategy, the brand manager must then introduce and explain the strategy to their staff. The brand manager and ABMs then communicate the brand values to employees in other departments across the company. They must also share the strategy to the outside partners and suppliers, such as advertising agencies and producers of TV commercials.

The brand manager and staff implement their strategy through a brand plan that includes such methods as paid advertising, social media, promotions, and public relations. They monitor their progress against the brand plan, and update the plan as needed. The brand manager's greatest challenge is often maintaining a consistent brand identify across all parts of the company and in all platforms where customers interact with that brand. They must also anticipate and implement any new needs that arise as the brand matures, as well as react to changes in the marketplace (such as new competition).

Marketing Director

Some brand managers move higher in the executive ranks by becoming marketing directors. The marketing director is responsible for the marketing business unit, coordinating and directing a group of brand managers and their subordinates.

They work directly with top executives, and may sit on the company's board of directors.

Marketing directors have more authority and more responsibility than brand managers. They have greater access to the financial and human resources needed to reach corporate goals, and greater independence in making decisions. They are held accountable for the financial performance of the entire portfolio of brands under their leadership. Marketing directors carry heavier workloads and face greater risks in meeting their performance objectives. They are also highly compensated for successfully meeting those challenges.

While fewer than 20 percent of brand managers move up to the director level, about 50 percent of ABMs become brand managers. Many brand managers are content to stay at that level, where their daily activities have a more direct impact on the success of the brands under their stewardship. Brand managers have the opportunity to work more closely with professionals from across the company on exciting, well-focused projects that improve the enterprise's bottom line while providing them immense personal satisfaction.

STORIES OF MARKETING PROFESSIONALS

I Am an Assistant Brand Manager

"I guess you could say I am following a traditional career path in brand management. My uncle ran a small advertising agency in Minnesota and I worked for him during the summers while I was in high school. Early on I knew I wanted to go into marketing, so I spent lots of time around my uncle's employees and customers, learning the basics. He also put me to work as a brand ambassador for some of his clients, like the local radio station and a small fast food chain in the Minneapolis suburbs. I also got plenty of sales experience by selling fruit for my high school band and ads for our yearbook.

After reviewing my educational options in the Midwest, I attended the University of Wisconsin in Madison and received my undergraduate degree in marketing. My BS (Bachelor of Science degree), plus my experience working with my uncle, helped me land a marketing research position with the Chicago office of a major consumer brands corporation. After several years attending part time, I completed my MBA at the University of Chicago and was promoted to assistant brand manager.

My workdays start around 7 a.m. and end in the early evening. I spend time checking emails, taking part in conference calls with cross-company teams, reviewing research compiled by marketing assistants, and supervising interns. I take steps every day to learn more about the business. I work on several of the consumer brands in the portfolio overseen by my brand manager, helping to fine-tune our strategy and keep pace with our competitors.

The part of my job I enjoy the most is working with social media, making sure that our brand image is consistent across all the different platforms on the Internet. I am also responsible for a major project to optimize our websites for smart phones and tablets. Our research finds that most of our target audience engages with our websites and social media pages through mobile computing, so we want to make sure we are interacting with our customers where they are most comfortable – and that they have a consistent brand experience no matter what type of technology they use.

I enjoy the work of being an assistant brand manager. I work with a great bunch of people and I'm learning something new every day. I continue to prepare for the day I can become a full-fledged brand manager with greater responsibilities."

I Am a Self-Employed Brand Management Consultant

"When I started my career more than 20 years ago, the discipline of brand manager was still evolving beyond its early roots in consumer packaged goods. I grew up in North Carolina and worked in our family business, where I found I had a flair for business. I enjoyed selling to our customers, but I was more interested in the strategic aspects of building a business than in the daily sales work. I decided to pursue a career in business administration while I explored my options for a career.

I started out at Duke University in Durham, North Carolina, where I majored in business administration and took a number of courses in marketing. After graduation, I stayed at Duke to attend the Fuqua School of Business at Duke, one of the top MBA business schools in the country. Much of my coursework centered on market research, and my MBA thesis focused on bringing branding concepts to the financial services industry.

With my graduate degree in hand, I decided to focus my job search on Charlotte, North Carolina, which is the center of the banking industry in the Southeastern United States. I soon landed a market research position with Wachovia, a regional banking chain that was just beginning to grow by acquiring smaller banks across the Southeast. After a couple of years in Charlotte, I was promoted to a brand management position with our main branch headquarters in Atlanta, Georgia.

At Wachovia, most of my work centered on enhancing the Wachovia brand and introducing it to new communities as we expanded our corporate footprint. Customer service had always been a priority throughout Wachovia's history, so we made that the focus of our brand image. Other "big banks" were also growing quickly by gobbling up competitors, but some of their business practices alienated customers at the institutions they bought, causing them to lose many of their customers. At Wachovia – despite our size — we treated our customers as individuals as a hometown community bank would do. From a branding standpoint, we made sure everything in the customer experience reflected those values and business practices that differentiated us from large banking conglomerates that seemed not to care about individuals. During my seven years at Wachovia, through dozens of acquisitions, we were successful in retaining acquired customers and increasing profitability, all measures that reflected well on our brand management techniques. As the company grew, I became head of Marketing Research and Development for Wachovia. However, despite our steady growth, the company ran into financial challenges during the banking crisis of 2008 and was acquired by Wells Fargo. The new owners wanted all their banks under the Wells Fargo logo, so we sadly bid farewell to the Wachovia brand we had built for many years.

After the transition to Wells Fargo, I decided it was a perfect time to pursue a long-time dream of opening my own company. I founded a consulting firm in Atlanta that works with existing brands to improve their performance and build a lasting legacy. We start with research and focus groups to define the current brand image and positioning, and then provide new strategies to move the brand towards the company's ultimate image. As much as I enjoyed my time at Wachovia, I feel running my own brand consultancy is the best job in the world. I get to work with all sorts of interesting people in a variety of industries. As the years go on, more and more businesses of all sizes are calling upon us to help them grow their brands."

PERSONAL QUALIFICATIONS

A SUCCESSFUL CAREER AS A MARKETING BRAND MANAGER DEMANDS BOTH TECHNICAL knowledge and positive personal characteristics. You can acquire the necessary skills – in branding techniques, business administration, marketing and advertising – through education. This provides a basis you expand with on-the-job training and work experience. Training plus real world experience familiarizes you with the tools, concepts and practical details of successful brand management.

These technical skills alone are not enough. You must also rely on solid personal traits – your habits, interpersonal skills, instincts, and learned behaviors. Some people find it easier to learn new technical skills than to modify those personal traits.

The successful brand manager relies on analytic skills, decisiveness, flexibility, thoroughness, integrity, leadership, curiosity, and an outgoing personality. Being able to define problems, analyze data, consider alternatives and find an optimal solution is critical to success. Creativity is also required to generate new ideas that benefit your company. Branding may seem like a "big picture" profession, but countless little pieces make up the image of a product or service, so you must also be a detail-oriented professional to master all the interrelated components.

You also need to be able to handle pressure and stress, because you are ultimately responsible for the success or failure of your brand. Expect to work long hours as you move into roles of higher responsibility. Branding executives must juggle multiple tasks while managing their time and budget effectively. You will be responsible for marketing strategy, as well as all aspects of a product – design, promotion, manufacturing, packaging, sales and financial profitability. As a manager, you are responsible not only for your own actions and decisions, but for those of the employees you lead, so brand managers spend a significant portion of their time mentoring team members.

Good writing and speaking communications skills are a must. You will deal with a number of professionals with different skills at varying levels of your organization. The brand manager is responsible for communicating the vision of what a brand means to other employees within the enterprise. You must also be able to put yourself in the position of your target customers while developing and implementing brand strategies. Learning a second language can also be useful, as an increasing number of products are targeting non-English speaking audiences. Regardless of your audience and the setting, you must be able to clearly outline details of opportunities, problems and proposed actions.

You must also be a good listener who is careful to understand the needs and concerns of colleagues, customers and upper level executives. At the same time, you must be persuasive, as any marketing position requires some degree of salesmanship.

Brand managers must keep up to date on the rapidly changing global marketplace. They must analyze industry trends so they can develop the most effective strategies to compete successfully. There is always something new to learn: new products and services, changes in computer technology, consumer research methods, and unique marketing techniques used by your competitors. If you are creative and flexible, you will be well positioned to succeed in brand management.

ATTRACTIVE FEATURES

LEADING A TEAM TOWARDS A COMMON goal is rewarding for many marketing brand managers. Brand managers have more authority, responsibility, and independence than the people who report to them. This higher responsibility brings better pay, prestigious titles, improved social standing, and perks such as generous travel budgets and business class airplane seats. Top executives are in a position to accomplish major successes that make the company money. They can gain the attention that may get them promoted to marketing director. Marketing brand managers are among the best-paid executives working in many industries.

If you like leading a team, solving problems, thinking creatively, and working within a variety of business disciplines, you should find this career both challenging and fulfilling. You will work with (and learn from) seasoned professionals as you bring your company's products and services to new markets, or build greater market share among targeted consumers. Your work will have a positive impact on your organization, your customers, and your employees.

Companies that employ marketing brand management professionals provide competitive salaries, attractive benefits, modern equipment, technical training, and many perks to help attract the best candidates to their workplace. Some even offer extra amenities like gym memberships and company retreats. These organizations also typically offer brand managers a well-defined path to move up the corporate ladder to positions of greater responsibility and increased compensation.

Marketing brand managers are held in high esteem by colleagues and top level executives in their own organization. Managers work closely with marketing peers, designers, copywriters, photographers, and other creative professionals from departments across the enterprise. A successful brand manager is highly valued within the corporate culture and faces excellent prospects for career advancement.

Brand managers enjoy pleasant working conditions. They spend most of their time in modern offices with up-to-date technology and a support staff to help them do their work. When they do travel, marketing managers may visit clients or attend conferences at exciting destinations around the world. While the position is challenging, most marketing brand managers enjoy the sense of accomplishment and the financial rewards that accompany success.

UNATTRACTIVE ASPECTS

WHILE MARKETING BRAND MANAGEMENT can be rewarding, it is also likely to be demanding and stressful. There are also more people seeking brand manager jobs than there are positions, so competition is keen to fill those jobs and advance along the career path.

The brand manager is ultimately responsible for the success of one or more brands – not just marketing, but also manufacturing, product quality, distribution, promotion, and ultimately, profitability. Managers must constantly be alert to threats to the brand's image, such as negative news reports or unhappy customers posting unfavorable reviews on social media. They must keep an eye on the competition, while implementing strategies and tactics to grow their own brand. Overall, constant pressure to succeed can bring physical and psychological stress.

Brand managers, assistant brand managers and marketing directors typically work more than 40 hours a week, including nights and weekends. Most managers are paid an annual salary rather than hourly wages, so working overtime without additional pay is expected. Those long hours can interfere with your personal life. Some managers enjoy traveling around the world, but others would prefer spending more time at home with their families.

Marketing managers also face the same challenges as other types of managers. The leader has to balance the needs of team members with the goals of the company, profit expectations, customer demands, and similar factors. Your team members will not always agree with your choices. A wrong decision that damages your brand can lose the company money, reduce returns for investors, and negatively affect your bonuses or chance for promotion. Thus, brand managers typically face more pressure (and more risk of losing their jobs) than managers in other types of positions.

Managers face constant demands to keep abreast with new developments in their industry and markets. When your company or competitors introduce new products and services, or when new government regulations affect your industry, you must learn about it, and communicate these changes to your team.

Managing a brand (or a family of brands) is a complex undertaking that demands a thorough knowledge of business administration. Most brands are too large for one person to handle, so you need to build a team with shared values and goals. You will be working with other departments that are responsible for manufacturing, distribution, advertising and selling products under the brand that you manage. The marketing brand manager must devise and communicate the strategy for the brand, and then make sure other departments work to support the intended brand image.

The daily work can be exhausting. Rolling out a new brand campaign, entering new markets, or crisis management to defend your brand from negative news, means working long hours for weeks at a time. The result is personal stress that sometimes leads to burnout. Brand managers typically juggle multiple tasks and maintain a hectic schedule. Even when an urgent project demands most of their time, they are still responsible for routine management duties, such as budgeting and employee performance reviews. Also, as with any career, you may have to deal with demanding managers, insubordinate employees, personality conflicts with peers, office politics, and difficult customers.

EDUCATION AND TRAINING

A CAREER AS A MARKETING BRAND manager requires at least a four-year college degree to get started. An undergraduate degree in marketing, business administration, advertising, or journalism provides a good entry point. However, employers will consider majors in almost any area, as long as you can demonstrate you have learned the key concepts of marketing and business administration. Your general business curriculum should include coursework in advertising, marketing, consumer behavior, statistics, finance, business law, market research, communications, accounting, economics, ethics and management theory. If you plan to focus on marketing within a certain industry, such as pharmaceuticals, technology or publishing, select appropriate courses for those sectors while learning all you can about business and marketing.

An undergraduate degree in marketing will not immediately bring you employment as a brand manager, but it can provide entry into positions that will prepare you for that role. Many future brand managers enter the workforce as marketing researchers, marketing coordinators, sales personnel, or marketing assistants. They may work in marketing, or they may be in sales, finance, or almost any other department. A marketing- or sales-related internship while you are still in high school or college can also provide useful experience, plus important connections that may be helpful when you enter the workplace. Employees who begin their careers from those entry-level positions can progress to roles of higher responsibility, however, the closer you get to full management roles, the greater the educational requirements.

Most companies require you to have (or be working towards) a Master of Business Administration degree to become an assistant brand manager. You usually need to complete your MBA to become a brand manager or marketing director. Some schools offer an MBA in brand management, while others include branding as part of MBA specializations such as advertising or marketing. Graduate-level branding courses include such essential components as brand targeting, brand positioning, product management, brand management, consumer behavior, and advanced market research.

The focus in a brand management-oriented MBA degree program is learning not only about the branding profession, but also about complementary fields that affect brand image and identity. Related courses include more in-depth classes on sales, promotions, advertising, media relations, and direct marketing. MBA coursework often includes strategic marketing, advanced market research techniques, international business, and consumer strategies. You will also need to learn general management theory and techniques, because brand managers function as executives who lead diverse teams of professionals.

Which schools should you attend for your undergraduate and graduate work? There are a variety of surveys that rank the top undergraduate and graduate schools for marketing careers. While attending a more prestigious school may give you a better shot at certain positions, many lesser-known colleges offer broad-based programs to help you start or advance your career.

Recent rankings by US News and World Report list these top colleges and universities for an undergraduate marketing degree:

University of Pennsylvania

University of Michigan-Ann Arbor

University of Texas-Austin

Indiana University-Bloomington

University of California-Berkley

University of North Carolina-Chapel Hill

New York University

University of Virginia

University of Wisconsin-Madison

University of Southern California

Bloomberg Businessweek ranks William & Mary as the best undergraduate business school for marketing in the United States. Washington University was second, followed by Virginia, Pennsylvania, Loyola, Cornell, Florida International, Arkansas, Elon and Michigan.

For graduate schools, US News and World Report ranks these top MBA programs:

Northwestern University

University of Pennsylvania

Stanford University

Duke University

Harvard University

University of Chicago

Columbia University

University of Michigan-Ann Arbor

University of California-Berkley

University of Texas-Austin

After college, you may be expected to take periodic continuing education to maintain and broaden your skills. This training could take place in a formal setting (such as company-sponsored classes) or in a less structured environment, such as online learning.

You may also decide to obtain a certification that demonstrates your knowledge and professionalism. Top marketing certifications include the American Marketing Association's Professional Certified Marketer program and the Certified Marketing Executive designation from Sales and Marketing Executives International.

EARNINGS

THE MEAN ANNUAL EARNINGS FOR marketing managers are estimated at about $130,000 annually, according to the most recent surveys. Note that this category includes brand managers as well as other marketing executives. Industry surveys generally find brand managers among the top paid marketing executives, particularly when they hold an MBA.

There are about 175,000 marketing managers, with a 15 percent growth in employment projected over the coming decade.

The top 10 percent of marketing managers by income earn more than $160,000 a year, while the lowest 10 percent are paid about $75,000.

The industries with the highest levels of employment for marketing managers include scientific and technical consulting services, computer systems design and related services, software publishers, and insurance carriers.

Earnings for marketing managers vary significantly by geographic region, type of industry, and local economic factors. The top-paying industry is financial services, with average earnings of almost $175,000. Other earnings leaders with average pay exceeding $160,000 include oil and gas extraction, securities and commodities firms, and scientific research and development.

The top-paying state for marketing managers is New York with a median salary of about $170,000, followed closely by the District of Columbia, New Jersey, Delaware and California.

Among brand managers, the consumer goods sector pays the highest salaries. The top pay goes to managers working in beauty, skin care and cosmetics; manufacturing and distribution; and wines and spirits. Marketing brand managers working in the apparel industry tend to have lower-than-average pay.

Entry-level marketing positions pay above the overall average for business openings. For example, many brand managers start out as brand ambassadors, product demonstrators and promoters who work through social media and at public events to promote a brand. They earn about $45,000 annually.

Keep in mind that the total value of an employment opportunity includes more than your salary the first day on the job. Performance bonuses can make up a large part of the compensation package, particularly for executives. Other benefits include medical insurance, paid time off, pensions and retirement funds, and stock purchase plans. Benefits at smaller firms tend to be less generous.

OPPORTUNITIES

THE CAREER OUTLOOK FOR MARKETING brand managers is expected to grow steadily for the foreseeable future. Employment of marketing managers is expected to grow about 15 percent by 2020.

Brand managers and other marketing executives play a key role in the growth of companies and other enterprises. Because marketing managers and their departments are important in an organization's revenue, marketing managers are less likely to be laid off than other types of managers, even in times of recession and economic downturns. Marketing managers will continue to be in demand as organizations seek to market their products to new customers and in more localities. Non-English speaking populations are expected to provide expanding markets. New products and services, as well as the continuing brands will need to be strengthened, meaning the need for savvy brand marketing managers will continue to grow.

There is strong competition for advertising, promotions, and marketing manager positions. These positions are highly desirable and are often sought by other managers and experienced professionals. The continued increase in Internet-based advertising and promotions, blogs, social media and mobile platforms means managers who can navigate the digital world should have the best prospects. Candidates with proven experience and leadership skills will also have an advantage over other prospective employees.

Most brand marketing management positions are found at large corporations, which are often headquartered in metropolitan areas. The states with the highest level of employment for marketing managers are California (about 30,000 jobs with a median annual salary of almost $150,000), followed by New York, Texas, Illinois and New Jersey. The metropolitan areas with the highest employment levels are New York, Los Angeles, Chicago, Minneapolis, Boston, Seattle, Washington, D.C., San Jose, Atlanta, and San Francisco.

Even working for a multinational corporation does not necessarily mean moving to a large city. Most have offices in mid-sized cities or in other areas close to their customers and/or manufacturing plants. Some brand managers travel across the country or internationally. Also, a growing number of companies are embracing telecommuting – working from one's home or another remote location far away from company headquarters. Companies report higher employee satisfaction and reduced operating costs when they implement telecommuting.

Brand management is a key component of many marketing positions found in cities of all sizes across the country. Potential employers include advertising and marketing agencies, medium-sized businesses, hospitals, government agencies, TV and radio stations, publishers, PR firms, and not-for-profit institutions. While small businesses and enterprises may not directly employ a brand manager, they may hire experts from marketing firms or independent, self-employed branding consultants.

GETTING STARTED

ARE YOU READY TO PURSUE A CAREER as a marketing brand manager? Making the decision is an important first step. Do not wait until you graduate from college to get started. There are many ways to take action now and start preparing for your future career.

Begin by gathering more detailed information about the different opportunities for brand managers, and how to position yourself to target your chosen sector. Books and periodicals about brand management careers can be found in libraries, from colleges and universities, and through your school's counselors. The Internet contains a wide range of easily accessible data from marketing firms, advertising agencies, media companies, government agencies, and professional associations.

Before college, find ways to get more experience in the marketing field. Actively seek out internship opportunities or entry-level jobs at marketing firms, non-profit organizations, and corporations with large marketing departments. Marketing classes are another great way to practice and improve your skills. There are local community college and online courses that expand your skills while you learn your craft. Keep your eyes open for chances to take part in marketing campaigns and promotions. Volunteer for leadership roles in clubs and other groups that give you a chance to develop your management skills. Get experience with sales — sell ads for the yearbook or take a part-time job as a salesperson.

A four-year degree with a major in marketing or business administration is needed to get started. A master's degree will help you move up to assistant brand manager. Investigate which colleges and universities can provide the required training for your future career. Make sure the schools you consider have programs that allow you to focus on branding, providing plenty of experience and marketing samples that can enhance your portfolio. It is common to start working after graduating from college and then pursue a master's degree part time, evenings and weekends.

Spend some time talking to brand managers and other marketing professionals, as well as those who work closely with marketers (such as copywriters, graphic designers or videographers). Ask brand managers what skills and experience will be most useful when you seek your first full-time position. You can find marketing professionals through professional associations or by contacting local firms. Industry associations can also be helpful for making contacts; learning about the profession and local career opportunities; and gaining inside information on internships, training programs, and scholarships.

Call on your personal network for support and advice. Discuss your plans with family and friends. Include your school counselor, who will share helpful information about local educational venues, employment prospects, internships, and networking outlets.

Once you gather your data, it is time to give careful thought to whether a career as a marketing brand manager feels right for you. Are you creative? Do you work well with others in a collaborative setting? Are you proficient with the technology? Can you work long hours to meet deadlines? Do you work well under pressure? Can you juggle multiple projects and keep everything moving forward? Are you comfortable in a leadership role helping a diverse group of people with different skills move towards a common goal?

Can visualize yourself happily pursuing a successful career as a brand manager. If so, start taking those first steps today towards a rewarding, fulfilling career!

ASSOCIATIONS

American Marketing Association
http://www.ama.com
American Association of Advertising Agencies
http://www.aaaa.org
Association of Product Management and Product Marketing
http://www.aippmm.com
ABrand Activation Association
http://www.baalink.org
Branded Content Marketing Association
http://www.bcmana.com
Business Marketing Association
http://www.marketing.org
Direct Marketing Association
http://www.thedma.com
Hospitality Sales and Marketing Association
http://www.hsmai.org
Internet Marketing Association
http://www.imanetwork.org
Mobile Marketing Association
http://www.mmaglobal.com
Sales and Marketing Executives International
http://www.smei.org
Web Marketing Association
http://www.webmarketingassociation.org

PERIODICALS

ABA Bank Marketing
http://www.aba.com
Advertising Age
http://www.adage.com
Adweek and Brandweek
http://www.adweek.com

B2B Magazine
http://www.b2bonline.com
Broadcast & Cable
http://www.broadcastingcable.com
iMarketing
www.imarketingmag.com
Journal of Brand Management
www.palgrave-journals.com
Marketing Insights
www.marketingpower.com
Search Engine Marketing Journal
www.searchenginemarketingjournal.com
Target Marketing
www.targetmarketingmag.com

WEBSITES

Bank Marketing News
www.bankmarketingnews.org
Brand Fever
http://www.brandfever.com
Branding Strategy Insider
www.brandingstrategyinsider.com
Brand Republic
http://www.brandrepublic.com
Interbrand
http://www.interbrand.com
Lippincott
http://www.lippencott.com/en
The Brand Renovator
http://www.brandrenovator.com
The Financial Brand
http://www.financialbrand.com

Copyright 2015

Institute For Career Research

Website www.careers-internet.org

For information on other Careers Reports please contact

service@careers-internet.org

Made in the USA
Lexington, KY
21 July 2018